Who Taught Ya About Money

5 Simple Steps to Bring The Bank aka Money to You

Paula Robertson Scott

ISBN: 978-0-578-36782-8

DEDICATION

My phenomenal mother Yvonne for everything she tried to teach me. My daughter Brianna who encouraged me and so many friends and family who encouraged me and believed that I had a story to share.

CONTENTS

ACKNOWLEDGMENTS

Many of my friends and family have always encouraged me to write a book like Jamillah, Brianna, and many more who need no mention. Walking into this journey has been trying but with your encouragement, I want to thank you. I would like to also acknowledge that my husband Alex made sure to help with giving me the space to write by not demanding too much of me. I just want to thank my mother for always teaching me and opening up my mind to learn more and more.

INTRODUCTION

Can I tell you how bomb ass you are for even picking this book up and taking your hard-earned cash and going online or at the register to buy my sweet, juicy book?

Now, tell the truth did you buy this book to be nosey? To see who taught me all this stuff or are you stepping up and putting yourself first? This book is about to rock your world with a tidbit of lessons I learned along the way and just to add some spice I added a bit of religious juice to help you on your path to be better with money.

All things go back to what you were taught and who taught you them. Tracking the steps back to when and where this lesson happened and was it helpful as you grew. Were there more lessons to learn or did you learn from watching others or did you have to learn from your own experience? Also, what weight it carried in your life.

Thank you again for traveling down memory lane with me and I know you will get something from this book that will make you a better being.

CHAPTER ONE MANIFEST

What does Manifestation have to do with Money? A lot if you learn the tool of Manifestation many things will come to you and even money. When I think about Manifestation, I think of who taught me about manifesting things. My first thought goes to the Oprah Winfrey Show where she discussed "The Secret." On the show, she discussed the book called "The Secret." She had a host of people on the Show who told their version of what The Secret was and how to achieve it. The author of The Secret was Rhonda Byrne who shared her story along with some other guests like Lisa Nichols, James Arthur Ray, Rev. Dr. Michael Beckwith, and Jack Canfield. They spoke about the Law of Attraction which most people are aware of in science class. It pretty much sums up that whatever you want you can attract it and the universe is constantly listening to us. Our thoughts, our actions, what we say. Also, the book gave you some sort of blueprint to get what you wanted. It fascinated me and I brought the CD version of the book years later.

For some reason, I thought that was who taught me about "The Secret." But in later years I read so many books chasing the secret and trying to understand it better that while reading Think and Grow Rich by Napoleon Hill I thought I have seen this book before. I was right. It was in college when I attended Clark Atlanta University, I recalled my peers reading this book because it was assigned to them by their professors. I was never assigned this book by my professor, so I guess I missed out.

So now at 47 years old, I am reading this book and questioned who came up with manifestation? I turned to the only source at my fingertips, which is Google. I then realized who was the first to teach me about manifesting your desires, and it was my Bible. Surprised? I am not because it comes full circle. I remember going to World Changers Church in Georgia and while Creflo Dollar preached going over words in the Bible like Matthew 17:20 "So Jesus said to them, "Because of your unbelief; for assuredly, I say to you, if you have faith as a mustard seed, you will say to this mountain, 'Move from here to there,' and it will move; and nothing will be impossible for you."

There were so many scriptures in the Bible it was as if they were just appearing because I was attracting them.

Here are a few I found:

Mark 9:23 "If thou can believe, all things are possible, to him that believeth."

Matthew 21:22 "And all things, whatsoever you shall ask in prayer, believing, you shall receive."

Matthew 7:7 "Ask, and it shall be given to you; seek, and you shall find; knock, and it shall be open unto you."

Proverbs 23:7 "As a man thinks in his heart, so is he."

One of my favorite scriptures is Habakkuk 2:3 "Write the vision. Make it clear on tablets so that anyone can read it quickly. For the vision is yet for an appointed time, but at the end it shall speak, and not lie: though it tarries, wait for it; because it will surely come, it will not be late."

The Bible talks about how to manifest what you want thru prayer, by writing it down.

So, there it was all the time, and growing up as a preacher's child and having a grandmother who is a preacher I was searching for the secret of manifestation, and it was right in front of me.

Surprisingly, I was practicing manifestation before I knew about The Secret in my younger years. I believed I manifested my good grades in school. I am not discrediting that I had to put in hours of studying. But I recalled a time in College at Long Island University in New York struggling with a math class and I honestly thought I was going to fail but I focused and prayed asking God and the Universe to help me to pass this class and I did with a grade of a C. I also recall I needed my transcript from a school and for some reason, they would not give it to me I would call numerous times and sent letters and the answer would be no. I would get discouraged and give up then a few weeks later it was nagging at me, and I would once again call and write letters, and eventually, I was able to get my transcript without paying anything additional. I believe the entire process took about 1 year and eight months.

There are many other things I asked the universe for and got. I asked for money, and it always seems I would get a windfall for enormous amounts of money. I asked for a promotion, and I got one. I even asked for a husband, and I am now married. I must say my method was similar to the book The Secret. I cut out words, vacation, money and pinned it to a board and I visualized what I wanted and some of the things I wanted to manifest took a couple of years to achieve but I eventually achieved them.

Surprise, surprise I wanted to see Oprah but never put it on my vision board. In my heart I desired it so much. I recalled one year in Atlanta I heard Oprah was here doing one of her tours for some Women's program, but I found out too late and could not get tickets. I was determined that the next time there was an opportunity to see Oprah I would. I saw where she did a cruise to Alaska, and I was ok missing that because I do not like the cold. I saw women on Instagram taking pictures of their time in the company of Oprah and Gayle. So, I followed her on Instagram and caught when she and Gayle announced a Girls Trip Cruise to the Caribbean. I shared it with my mom, aunts, cousins, and friends and booked our trip to see her. We were soooooooooooooo excited. The day we were boarding the Ship we were accompanied by other excited women, and some had their men who they name, their Gayle. Everyone had a Gayle and a story to tell. I was here with some of the most important people in my life, my mom, aunt, and cousin.

We saw Gayle the first day and we were so close we could reach out and touch her. We enjoyed the activities from yoga, comedy, meditation, dancing to the band. The food on the cruise was great they even had a gluten-free option which I was surprised by the various selections.

So, we kept missing Oprah which left some of my party disappointed. On the day that Oprah spoke to my group and countless other women, I felt full of knowledge. Even though I did not get to personally meet her my destiny was not to meet her but to be in her presence and get the "WORD." The WORD was the knowledge that she shared with us, and I was full and satisfied. She filled my brain with so much knowledge, she just poured into us.

I know some of my friends who would throw away their vision boards each year and create a new one, but I always thought what about the things that you did not achieve yet? Were they thrown away too? Were they lost and forgotten dreams and goals? Therefore, I keep mine until each thing is accomplished or achieved, then I remove it from my vision board until it is empty and then start it all over again with new items, and words.

My mother will usually say things to me and leads me down the road to wonder and deeply think about what she has said. One day she said when you say something it usually happens. I decided to pay close attention to what I said, and I realized my mother was correct. So, I then became incredibly careful of what I said. What I put out in the Universe because I would be scared if it is not good and I said it to someone, then it would transpire. I tend to talk a lot, so this gift has made me more self-aware and a lot of times I refrain from saying or giving my opinion on things because if it is not good and it happens, I feel sorry for whoever I was giving my opinion too. I also realized sometimes I do not have to speak it, but I may hold my opinion to myself but all the time someone is talking I am thinking about it and then a few days later they will tell me the end result and I usually will say I was thinking that, but I didn't want to say it and put it out in the Universe. Now, I do not always think bad thoughts. I have told a coworker when I was out to dinner that her boyfriend is the person she will be married to and months later there was a proposal. Come to think of it I have told a couple of my female coworkers and friends that they would marry a particular guy or have a baby or some other future happy event in their lives.

I share this to say that what we think and say holds weight in our Universe, and you will be surprised by the power you hold within yourself. What I love the most about the Bible is that it tells you are worthy and that you have something special within you some extraordinary gifts and it can be found on:

1 Corinthians 12:7 "To each is given the manifestation of the Spirit of the common good. 8-11 For to one is given by the Spirit the word of wisdom; to another the word of knowledge by the same Spirit; To another faith by the same Spirit; to another the gifts of healing by the same Spirit; To another the working of miracles, to another prophecy; to another discerning of spirits; to another divers kinds of tongues; to another the interpretation of tongues; But all these worketh that one and the selfsame Spirit, dividing to every man severally as he will."

When my daughter was a teen, I taught her about The Secret and had her create a vision board. Like most teens, she was not interested but as an adult, she has adopted the teaching of The Secret, and now she is a master at it. She is so intuitive and 9 out of 10 things that she writes down or puts on the vision board she has accomplished. She has truly tapped into her gifts from the Universe. She started her business by manifesting and has grown it as well as multiple streams of revenue by practicing manifestation.

While I was dating my husband, I share The Secret CDs with him. Funny thing he still has those CDs and will not let me loan them out to my friends. He really thought it was his little secret. We made vision boards. He believed in it but did not practice it much, so his success rate is less than my daughters and mine. However, we do practice family manifestation exercises. We look for signs from the Universe like Billboards, Street Signs, Words on social media. We also hide money so people can find it and eventually it comes back to us. We write stuff in our manifestation journals and try to focus on it weekly.

Our parents and close relatives and friends shape us. Like many, most of what I was taught came from my parents. My mother is an extraordinary woman and she taught me the best she knew how to. Similar to most people her experiences shaped her good or bad. She was the first person to teach me about fear. I recall getting into trouble at an early age and being fearful, sometimes terrified about the discipline that was to come. My mother is not perfect, and she did not know how to handle her stressors, so it was taken out on me. Being a Caribbean woman, she then blamed me and labeled me the "bad child" when in actuality, it was a lack of knowledge and help from her circle which led to these extreme punishments.

So, fear crept in, and I was fearful of punishment. When I did wrong, I was fearful of being caught then later in life fear took over. On 9/11 fear took over my whole life. Working at the World Trade Center in Manhattan, New York on 9/11 and that building being targeted for a terrorist attack fear ran rapid in my mind. I feared that I would not make it out. I feared for the other victims that jump from the building to their deaths. I feared trying to cross the bridge between Manhattan and Brooklyn thinking the terrorist would bomb the bridge as I walked over it trying to get home. I feared for my daughter and then once arriving home I feared every noise, siren. So, I ran, ran straight to the safety of Florida where my parents relocated to. However, I still had this crippling fear, fear that my back pain and mental state would never be the same, and it has not. It has gotten better but never the same. I recalled Creflo Dollar speaking about fear and I brought his book about how to overcome fear. He laid out many biblical scriptures and with consistent therapy, I was able to get some ease from fear.

I learned how fear can stop your manifestations right in its tracks. Fear blocks your wishes and goals for your life, and it can creep in and block all your blessings. So do not have fear when manifesting your dreams and hopes for your life. Believe, believe in yourself and your dreams for your future. Believe in your goals. I lean on these Bible scriptures to reinforce not to have fear but faith.

2 Timothy 1:7 "For God gave us a spirit not of fear but of power and love and self-control."

Psalm 27:1 "The LORD is my light and my salvation; whom shall I fear?"

I recall Angela Simmons, Reverend Run's daughter posting this scripture and it moved me Matthew 6: 25-26. I felt empowered and it changed me.

Matthew 6:25-26 "Therefore I say unto you, Take no thought for your life, what ye shall eat, or what ye shall drink; nor yet for your body, what ye shall put on. Is not the life more than meat, and the body than raiment? Behold the fowls of the air: for they sow not, neither do they reap, nor gather into barns; yet your heavenly Father feedeth them. Are ye not much better than they?"

So now I manifest with faith that whatever I want I will receive it. If I do not receive it when I want it, I then know sometimes plans do not work out because God has something better that he has prepared for us. Knowing that everything is in God's timing and God's will. Block out the naysayers because they cannot stop God's plans for you. In life, you will be surprised who your cheerleaders are and how many you have. I was and still am.

Remember to practice your manifestation exercises. Write it down each day and put-up images of what you want. Put it out to the Universe. Become laser-focused on what you desire. For instance, put pictures of your desires on your lock screen on your phone, put the pictures on your desk. Or on your bathroom mirror. Also, make room in your life for your desires. What do I mean by that? If you want another car, make room in your garage for another car, if you want a partner/spouse make room in your home for that. Remove things that will block it. Focus on you.

One important thing too, KARMA! Remember if you want things in life you have to have a good attitude, treat people kindly and do good deeds. Be intentional because if you do bad things, it will eventually come back to you and BLOCK what you're manifesting. Or what you have manifested example money, you will get it and LOSE it.

CHAPTER TWO MONEY

Money aka The Bank! We all want it and for those who do not have enough, we want the secret of how to get more. Those who have it, they just want to sustain it. I am the other that wants more but just enough for me and to help my family. Fame is not what I desire but just enough, just to be a millionaire and I believe I am on track. I set out a course to travel to achieve this.

So, who taught me about Money? Once again, the prize goes to my mother. I am remembering seeing her put money under her chest of draws when I was about 7 or 8 years old. I did not really have a burning desire for money at that age but in Jamaica, I knew I could use it to buy Kentucky Fried Chicken, KFC. In Jamaica at that time most people cooked and did not really eat out unless it is a special occasion. Just a note, the home-cooked food was better in taste and quality than fast food or fancy restaurant food. But I still wanted it. So, I looked under her dresser and took my mother's money. Well, I just took twenty dollars. I did not realize at that time that I was stealing but that is what it was. I would take that twenty dollars and buy KFC and it was so good.

Later when I visited my aunt and uncle in Queens, New York I took or aka stole their money too. Usually, it was twenty dollars every day to buy candy. Unlike taking twenty dollars once from my mother's stash, I knew this was wrong and I deserved the punishment I received. For some reason taking that money from my mom did not correlate as something wrong to me. I then picked up the nasty habit of lying which years later I had a disdain for, and I try my best to not lie, or I will avoid the question rather than lie. I also stop the habit of taking aka stealing money from anyone.

I remember my mother telling me she had a savings account for me when I was in high school. I would withdraw the money and take my classmates to lunch. Until it was almost gone. I really did not understand the value of a dollar and how hard one worked to achieve it. My father tried to teach me in my teenage years. He gave my siblings and I allowance. However, he gave me more allowance than my mother did. He gave me fifty dollars a week from working in his store. Every time I would get my allowance, I would ask my dad or one of my sisters to take me to the mall and I would spend ninety percent of the allowance on clothes for when I go back to New York to my mother. My dad the preacher, believed women should not wear pants or short skirts to expose their skin. I brought these items to take back to New York to wear, where there were no rules on women's clothing by my mother. I would buy ice cream or snacks with the rest of my allowance. My dad made us pay for snacks out of his store with our allowance. He used to say, "you are not going to eat out my profits." So as soon as I got my allowance it was all spent, and he would not give me anymore. Therefore, I would ask my middle sister to give me some of her money or buy me a snack and she usually would. Thank you, Alice.

At age 15 or 16 I got a job and no longer needed an allowance from anyone. I was always a hard worker and leader. I just did not realize I was a leader back then. At age 18 I felt obligated to work and move out on my own, so I worked as a dancer, and this is where I learned to budget. I had to pay my own bills because I was on my own and I had to save the money I had. My best friend at the time told me about Clark Atlanta University and without knowing it I manifested going there so I had to save my money to pay for room and board and school. I did that and money became so important.

Earning more money became more important than having it. So, I thought an education like a four-year degree would do that for me. I had mediocre jobs like a cashier and then later I worked in marketing research. But Clark Atlanta University was expensive, and I worried about paying for school. My dad was not any help and my aunt Norma tried to help me. I eventually stop going to school. I returned to New York unhappy and tried to find a new path, so I worked then eventually dated and had my daughter. Then I hopped back to Georgia where I work for a telecom company and made a great wage. However, that was not where I wanted to be, so I returned to New York and struggled. I mean struggled, I went on welfare and got food stamps for two months, and then I realized that life is not for me. I need real money!

I began working at Macys as a seasonal worker and manifested a permanent position and I got that. Then I needed more money, so I worked as a vendor for a well-known designer brand and the money was better, but I wanted to make something comparable to what I made at the telecommunication company in Atlanta, and bam! I manifested a wonderful job at a high-end stationery store. I went from the stationary store to another telecom company then I landed what I thought was the perfect position with great wage at a famous health insurance company at the World Trade Center.

I began reading books from Suze Orman after seeing her on TV and on The Oprah Show. Suze Orman spoke about budgeting and debt on TV. I was a good pupil because I would write in my planner my bills and when they needed to be paid. I finally achieved what I manifested but who would have thought that 9/11 would happen. I knew having a degree at the time would bring me more money, so I started back on track to get that degree from Long Island University all so known as LIU in Brooklyn, and everything was going great until 9/11.

When I returned to Florida, and I worked on finishing up my degree from LIU. I went to a University in Florida that transferred my grades to LIU. Once I got my degree and was looking for a job, I initially had no luck in the banking industry and then I got a job that was giving me all the money. Well, that is what I believed at the time. I landed at another telecom company and there were many ways to make extra money. I lived comfortably and thought I had enough money and spent accordingly. On Fridays I treated my parents and adopted siblings to dinner, I lived in a comfortable apartment and drove a nice car, a Nissan. I thought life was good and it was, but it could be better.

I received a windfall of money from the 9/11 disaster, and I could buy whatever I wanted but did not. I decided to leave my job and relocated to Atlanta and brought a couple of houses. I furnished my house with whatever I desired, and money made it happen. I started a business and made some money. Then the money was running out due to the recession and my business was not bringing in the profit I projected, and I had to get a job. So, I went back to the telecom company and the money was good. Then at one point, I thought about getting the "I MADE IT CAR" which in my eyes it was a BMW for most people. Suddenly, I had a thought it was just a "thing." I can always get it I do not need to get this vehicle to announce to the world I have made it, or I have arrived. I continued to work and struggled at times. I would read David Bach The Automatic Millionaire and it gave me a new spin on Money. I moved up in the telecom company and as I aged, I realized that this company was laying off more and more workers each year. Therefore, I had to start taking money seriously. I then started reading Dave Ramsey The Total Money Makeover. I realized the ones who had it could just retire with ease from my company and the ones who did not, had to continue working. I took notice of the ages of my peers. There was one guy who was 70 who was still working. This was because he did not have enough money to retire. This guy eventually retired after doing a check-up on his portfolio and with his wife's approval.

I saw some more of my older peers that the younger peers were questioning "why they haven't retired yet?" As if they were trying to push them out the doors. Which I thought was hilarious because you do not know their situations and who made you all the judge of who needs to retire now? I kept thinking does it make you all any difference, does it put money in your account? Well, it did. Because my younger peers were fearful that if the older colleagues did not retire then the younger ones would be selected to be on the surplus list. Which was not really how the company selected people. But money became super important for me. It was around this time when I really took a look at my 401K to see if I had enough to retire. I received advice

from my peer to take advantage of the company-sponsored financial advisors and they were able to oversee my investment and suggest or move my investment accordingly to make more of a profit. After reading multiple financial books and magazines there is a common trend that if you have a financial advisor managing your money it will usually produce higher yields. I also reviewed my budget and cut some costs like eating out a lot. I worked with my advisor on my projected future goal of becoming a millionaire that I am currently manifesting.

There were many things that I have learned about money even with this current covid pandemic. I took a course with Coursera called The Science Of Well-being from Yale and it discussed what you needed to be happy. I initially thought it was money! But it's not. I thought like most, if you have more money, you can buy more things to make you happy. I was wrong. I learned experiences are what stays in your mind forever not money, not the things that money can buy. Like for instance celebrating a birthday with family, going on vacations with friends. You will tend to forget about the red bottoms you brought or the expensive purse you were gifted. The course also talked about the sweet number all so known as the happiness salary which apparently at the time of the study it was $75K a year. Apparently, if you make anything over $75K per year, it does not make you happier. You can buy more stuff and have nicer things, but you will not be happier than someone who makes $50K or $250K per year. The choice was easy I chose Happiness! I am intentional when someone's birthday comes around, I do not buy gifts I buy experiences because that will last longer than any expensive gift, I give them. For my mother's birthday, I took her to Africa, and she still speaks about that trip. For my daughter's birthday, I took her to Mexico, and on the day of her birthday, she had many wonderful experiences from balloons and rose petals in her room to our friends accompanying her to a theme restaurant. Which was enjoyable for the whole group. For my friend's birthday I paid for a custom yard sign with things she enjoyed then we went to dinner.

When thinking of money, one cannot help but think about wealth. Who does not want to be wealthy? I think about being rich quite often. I know I will be a millionaire someday because I will it. But I think more about what I will leave for my family. I am laser-focused on this like the Bible says, Proverbs 13:22 – "A good man leaveth an inheritance to his children's children: and the wealth of the sinner is laid up for the just." So, I will make sure I leave enough for my children's children. It is only right.

I also learned more recently since the pandemic from my daughter that you do not have to have a degree to have wealth or money. I believe I knew that but did not know many people who accomplished this. I grew up being told you need a degree to make it to live a good life. I instilled this in my daughter. She was accepted to a top University and would stop her formal education from time to time. She took the knowledge she learned from working and did her research and started her own company where she makes more money than some people with a four-year degree. Well, she showed me. I have two degrees and as a brown skin girl, I am not making what I should be making in the corporate world. This is not for lack of trying. So, this dream of a degree giving you all these benefits, unfortunately, it's not giving me that. I am not going to say it has not opened some doors for me but there are so many entrepreneurs without a degree that are blowing past me. Therefore, I decided to get in the race to make it on my own.

Having money is one thing, learning to live within your means is another. I remember in my past dating this guy who I thought was so fabulous. I initially thought he was the prize. He made a lot of money. My wage was substantially less than his. He had a fabulous house, drove an expensive car. Was fine as hell. Everything on the surface that I wanted. He dressed well and smelled good too. But the dude was broke! What I mean by that is he had made a great salary, but he did not live within his means. He could not afford the life he lived. We were dating and spoke of marriage. I was terrified because I kept thinking he would take the money I earned and spend that too. He even borrowed money from me and to this day never paid it back. During our relationship, I realized that he was competing with me. See, I had a windfall of money and even though I made less than him I managed my money wisely. Do not get me wrong I was not the perfect budgeter, but I had enough sense to live within my means. With the windfall, I brought an additional property, and he noticed my money moves. As a man, he wanted or felt he should be making those types of financial moves also. So, during the recession, he brought another house and took the money out of the home. Eventually sometime after we broke up, he was in bankruptcy court because he could not manage his bills. Years later he told me he got married but was still checking for me. He also told me he was surplus from his job. The woman he married she had money. I am not saying he married her for money, but you draw your own conclusion.

One way to hold on to your money is to create a budget and stick to it. Listen, it takes practice, but I believe after 3 months of creating a budget it will become a habit. One of the things that are quite common with most people's budget is eating out and that usually takes a substantial chunk of your budget once you have set and used a budget for three months you can see where you will need to cut like for instance not eating out as much or shopping online/or instore to save some money. I know a big one is Amazon;

many people love to shop on Amazon, and they make it so easy. I actually love shopping on Amazon but like most of yall, I have to be careful not to overspend. Another tactic is to go to your bank account. Most banks now have a spending summary on checking accounts and credit cards. If you cannot locate it online or on your app, call your bank and ask them where you can find it online. It will show you how much you're spending and where you're spending it on. There are so many budget apps like Mint, Everydollar, YNAB. Or you can do a spreadsheet or the old fashion way paper or pen/pencil.

CHAPTER THREE DEBT

We cannot romanticize the future without remembering the past. This is my thought on debt. The subject of Debt appears in the Bible numerous times, but my two favorites are:

Deuteronomy 15:1-2 "At the end of every seven years thou shalt make a release. And this is the manner of the release: Every creditor that lendeth ought unto his neighbor shall release it; he shall not exact it of his neighbour, or of his brother; because it is called the Lord's release."

Proverbs 22:7 "The rich ruleth over the poor, and the borrower is servant to the lender."

The latter one can be heard on The Dave Ramsey Show numerous times. He quotes this and it resonated with me. Who wants to be a slave? No one! But we do this all the time when we charge on our credit card and pay monthly payments with interest. Or when we take out a Car, Mortgage, and personal/business loans. We make these monthly payments and pay these lenders interest.

I recently told my husband we do not own our home. He looked perplexed because, we pay the mortgage every month. We pay the taxes and insurance so what did I mean we do not own our home? I have lived in this home for 16 years, but it was not mine. Literally! If you have a loan aka mortgage on your home, you do not own it. The bank owns your home, and they can take it whenever they feel like it. However, if you make timely monthly payments that usually does not occur. It is the same for your vehicle if your making payments and have a loan. You do not own it until it's paid off. So, in a sense, we are slaves to the lender. The sad part is some people lose their possessions example houses, cars after paying for them for numerous years and miss a few payments, what a waste. This is just how debt works right?

I found the 1st scripture Deuteronomy 15:1-2 when I was working on paying off my debt and I looked at my credit score. I was curious what made up the properties of the Fico Score. I realize 35% was based on your payment history if you paid your debts on time and 30% was based on how much you owed and how much of your available credit have you used. I then realized that the credit score was based solely on debt. I was so angry and felt duped. Why do we even rely on a credit score? The funny thing about it is, if you do not have any debt or if you are paying off your debts eventually, after some time, your credit score starts dropping. You will then have a low credit score because you do not have any debts.

I then finally got it; this is why they offer you credit cards when you are in college. The fraud is to allure you into getting debt. Think about it initially you had no debts but now they are enticing you to get some debt to gain a credit score. How ludicrous! I have to laugh at myself for being so dumb. This is a case where if they say it enough times you start to believe it to be true. Kind of like if the President says the White House is green enough times and your Teachers, Parents, and Leaders who you admire and look up to keep saying the White House is green soon you start to believe its green too.

So, you may be thinking then how do I get my assets like a house or car? Well, when Dave Ramsey kept saying you do not need a credit score to own a house and suggested a company that he promotes who will give you a loan without a credit score it now made more sense. Because I ultimately did not agree at first nor did I understand. Now back to the Scripture, when I thought about the credit score and the statute of limitations of seven years, I wondered did that originally come from this Bible Scripture. I also, wondered when debtors reach out to family members to pay the debt of someone who passed did it come from the Bible as well.

So, you may be wondering who taught me about debt. Well, it was school. The pesky people who set up shop on the college campus and lure you into getting a credit card. Yeah, those people. They give you these cards but really do not give you instructions. Just pay it when your bill is due. But they do not advise you not to purchase more than you make and what happens when you are unable to pay. Haha, they probably do this because if they told you the hard facts this little fishy would RUN. Yes, run far away from debt.

I have been in debt more than once I guess; I did not learn the first time. After reading those books on debt I made settlements as I stated earlier and got rid of my debt. Then I ran those credit cards up later in life and struggled to pay them. I was living above my means and giving the debtors all the interest. I was also the definition of insanity. Well, let's go back to manifestation, the second time around I got a windfall of money and paid off my credit card debts and promise myself not to get myself in that situation again. No more credit card debt. I helped my husband when we got married to get out of debt again more than once. At one point he even had a higher credit score than mine due to us working to get rid of all his debt. We utilized the same methods of making settlements due to them being close to the "**Lord's Release**" of seven years. Now, most books on debt advise you to pay the whole debt off and that looks better on your Credit Report. However, we did not want to use all our funds, or we did not have the value of the whole debt, so a settlement was the most favorable option and it still resulted in an increase of the credit score. Even though I am not a fan of credit I am aware in my world you are looked at more favorable when you have a high credit score. So, I play the credit score game. I use my credit cards for groceries, gas, shopping, and paying utilities and I pay the bill off before it's due so that my credit score goes up and I am not charged any interest. But there is an art to this, and you must be diligent. If I charge something on the 14th of the month, I make sure to pay it off before the 14th of the following month so that I am not charged any interest. When I first started doing this, I was charged interest twice before I got the hang of it but because I was a good customer the credit card companies waived the charges for me, this is why I stated you must be diligent so that you will not be charged any interest.

I recall my husband saying to me you pay your bills different from how my mother pays her bills. I thought this was interesting, and I asked how so? He said you pay all the bills in full when they come in where my mother pays a partial amount. I also asked his sister who is a professional in New York if she paid her bills the same as her mom and she said yes. I really started thinking we also learn how to manage our debt payments from our parents. I am not sure who taught me to pay my bills in full, but I just thought that's how it's done, but I guess this just applies to some people and not all. But come to think about it I have always been that person that does things pretty much by the books. I would have never thought to purposely not pay the whole bill unless I just did not have the funds. I even remember when I brought my first couple of properties when the mortgage statement came and said the mortgage was due on the 1st, I paid it on the 1st. Until my girlfriend said you need to pay it on the 15th because it is late on the 16th then I changed the way I pay my mortgage. Things have now changed I pay it on the 16th because now it's late on the 17th. I also learned that if they give you grace take it. Another thing I learned was that when you pay it early the companies are gaining interest on your money where you are not. So, the 1st -14th I get the interest, and then I pay it on the date it's due before it's late.

I remember the last recession in 2008 everyone was getting a mortgage forbearance and then in the end they moved the missing mortgage payments to the end of the loan as a mortgage modification. Well, I wanted that same grace as well. At the time, my mortgage was with Chase, and I called them, and they told me I could not get the same grace as other homeowners because I paid on time. Is that ridiculous? I thought that was so crazy, I was struggling to pay my mortgage at this time, but I was being penalized for paying my mortgage on time. So, I applied another strategy and was eventually granted a modification. I am never going to tell you not to pay your debts on time but sometimes you have to apply a little pressure and use good judgment to get what you want.

Being in debt can be so embarrassing. Most people would never divulge that they are in debt. In today's society as a single person when dating or even a married couple, society would look down on you for being in debt and not doing something about it. I genuinely believe America thrives on debt. This is why people pose or flex like they have more than what they really have, and this goes along with the saying stop trying to keep up with the Joneses because the Joneses are broke. In Georgia you see a lot of that, people will drive the most expensive car but do not have a place to live. Or they are renting these automobiles or doing the subscription service where you pay say between $550 -$1,200 depending on the type of automobiles and you get to change the vehicles twice a month and this covers your insurance and the monthly payments, but you do not own the vehicles. Also, people here will be living in a mansion with no furniture or renting a mansion but pretending to own said property. Listen, do not believe the hype it's all fake.

There are so many tools to get you into debt. But I have also seen cases like in Jewish, Muslim, and Christian cultural settings where you can borrow money without interest. I personally do not like to borrow because I hate paying back so I rather stack my Benjamins than borrow.

So how do we get out of debt? Some people follow the snowball method which pretty much is lining up all debt from smallest to largest. Then pay off the smallest and then take the money you used to pay the smallest debt and put it towards the next debt in line to make a bigger payment and this will allow you to pay the debt off faster. This step is repeated until you get to the largest debt and then you have completed paying off the debt. The other method I have heard of is the avalanche method where you make payments to all accounts and the debt with the highest interest rate you put extra payments towards until you pay it off then move on to the next debt with the highest interest rate.

Then I read about making debt payments automatic. I actually like that method because you never miss a payment but my preferred way to pay off debt is the debt snowball because it makes more sense to me. It reminds me of the saying that you can "eat an elephant one bite at a time" by Desmond Tutu. It just seems more feasible in my case. I think the avalanche method takes longer for you to see results and there is not a sense of accomplishment that will not keep you motivated to accomplish your goal. But this is just my opinion.

Debt is such a big issue, the most popular ones are credit card debt, home loan debt, automobile debt, and the most hated, well by me is student loan debt. Currently, the whole United States of America is waiting to see what

President Joe Biden is going to do about student loan debt including me. We Need Help! America has made it so normal to borrow money to go to school which in turn has made it into an overwhelming problem. People owe so much in student loan debt that the debt that is owed is sometimes equivalent to a home loan, this is ridiculous! Even the part that it sometimes takes more than half a lifetime to pay off this debt. Listen, I am at a loss with this the only thing I can think of to do is write my congressmen/women, Senators, and President. Appeal to them about this ever-growing concern. But in the meantime, while they have this pause, where we are not accruing interest. I am still paying my debt because this is who I am, I pay. Remember, me telling you earlier I like the debt snowball method, and this is currently my last debt with the exception of my home loan.

CHAPTER FOUR SAVING AND INVESTING

Dave Bach states to make saving automatic and yes that is who taught me something about investing and saving. But when I worked at a health insurance company, I learned about investing in my 401k. Just like most people I just put away some money, but I did not know how to allocate it. I think maybe it was 4-5 percent at first that I invested but I never diversified it, nor did I watch to see if it grew. I was clueless.

I later learned to invest in a Mutual Fund. Now, I am not a financial advisor, and I was doing what I was told in the many books I have read. But people like myself did not know which type of Mutual-Fund one should you invest in. Well, this is where you ask the questions to your Fidelity, Vanguard, Morgan-Stanley, or your local bank. However, I frown on going to your local bank but go to the experts that primarily deal with investments. Ask them what Stock, Bonds, and other Securities are in the Mutual Fund? What makes up the Portfolio? Choose the one that has the flavor you like but generally, the experts suggest that Mutual Funds should be diversified with Growth, Aggressive Growth, Growth and Income, and International. But it's your job to ask the tough questions again what names of Stocks, Bonds, and Securities are in the Mutual Fund.

Another thing that has piqued my interest is Index Funds they mirror the S&P 500 and the way it was told to me is that you get a percentage of the actual Share you want. If you want Apple Stock you would not own the whole Stock but a percentage of it in the Index Fund. Most of the time it beats the S&P 500 with the interest that it makes. Again, there are many flavors out there, so you have to ask questions. Like for instance if I wanted one, with a Portfolio with Tesla, Google, GM, etc. I would ask the Financial Advisor to show me what is in the Portfolio or Prospectus.

One particularly important thing is that you want to look at the track record of anything you invest in. Look at the 10 yr. Return. If the investment has not been around that long, then extend your view to however many years that it has been in the market to see the rate of return and the volatility. Fees, yes Fees, ask the advisors or the companies example Vanguard, Fidelity what are the fees they plan on charging you? With the new FIRE – Financial Independence Retire Early movement, no one wants to pay enormous fees. We do not like anything over 1% and they need to be a fiduciary, meaning they have your interest in mind not just to take your money from you.

I am a firm believer in paying myself 1st. We all have bills. When I receive my pay, before I pay my bills, I take out a percentage for myself. I refuse to make these big companies (Walmart, Amazon, Publix, Macy's) family members rich. Without me getting a piece of the pot, of my hard-earned money.

My mother is a great saver she would do a partner a well-known saving program in the Caribbean where a group of people gets together to save a sum of money over a certain amount of time. So, say there are 10 people who are trying to save $1,000 over 10 weeks. Let's do the math, that would be $100 over 10 weeks. Then each person takes a number the person with number 1 gets a draw meaning they collect their 1st $1,000 on the 1st week. Then the next week the person with number 2 collects their draw. However, the people in the group agree to continue to pay and stay in the group for a total of 10 weeks until everyone gets their draw. A partner is also known as a sou-sou among distinct groups and was adopted during the covid pandemic by some American people, but most were doing it as a fraud and not everyone got their draw.

I like a partner, but I do not like that you do not get any interest on your money like you would if you saved it in a bank. Like in a high yield saving account. Or in the stock market where depending on if you invest it in a good stock, you can grow interest. Also, with a partner, you have to pay the person who holds the money, and it is generally higher than the fee you pay the bank to hold your money. So, I respect people who are in a legitimate partner or sou-sou because you really can save but you are not making interest on your money. There is also, the trust factor that the person running the partner is not going to run off with your money. At least in the bank, my money is insured up to a certain amount.

This happened when I worked at Macy's Herald Square in New York City also known as Manhattan. I recalled a manager who was from the Caribbean, and she started a sou-sou. She approached other managers and subordinates about joining the sou-sou. She approached me and asked me if I would join, and I told her I was not interested. About a week or two there was a scandal at Macy's. Someone did not get their draw and it circulated the store like wildfire. I do recall this Manager got reprimanded and they told her she could not do this in the store and that she should have known better to involve her subordinate because it would be a hardship on them if they lost their money.

Ha Ha well, that's at least what I heard but who knows what really happened.

I recently visited my mother, and she always has the tendency to tell me how much she saved on an item. She will say, guess how much I paid for this shirt? I usually say I do not know. With glee on her face, she will say something like 5 dollars. Then throughout my visit, she mentioned other things she believed she got a discount on. She usually adds I got it at a thrift store or Costco or maybe Marshall/TJ Maxx etc. Now, my mother has a lot of clothes, shoes, etc. She does not need anything. During one of these conversations, I said to her "IT'S NOT SAVING IF YOU'RE SPENDING." Then I laughed and told her I was going to put that in my book. A great way to SAVE is to STOP SPENDING! Stop buying stuff you do not need. Just because you have money in the bank that is not a reason to spend frivolously. I believe in my mother's case it would be best if she saved that money for retirement. See, she will be retiring soon, and I just think the money she spent today on these frivolous things she could be earning interest on for tomorrow, tomorrow being retirement.

In the books I mentioned before written by Suze Orman, David Bach, and Dave Ramsey, they always advise you to save. Even jobs now advise you to save and invest. If you have a 401k, they advise you to save 15% and an additional 5%. The goal is to constantly increase your saving rate, some people are even able to save up to 50% -75% of their income. However, they just do not save it in a basic savings account they look for a Money Market Account or a Brokerage Account and stash it in an IRA. Where you can grow interest. The IRA will help you to grow compound interest repeatedly by putting money in investments that in a thriving market will go up and in a low market there may be some losses. But let's be truthful 15% is hard for most to save. I always suggest starting small try 5% and keep adjusting it until you get to 10% then 15%. However, if your organization gives you a match always start investing at that match so you can get the money you deserve and earned from your company. So, if they match at 6% start investing 6% and GET THAT MONEY YOU DESERVE AND WORKED HARD FOR! A wonderful way to continue to increase your saving rate is whenever you get a raise keep increasing your saving rate by 1% until it grows to 15%.

I recently coined the phrase COOL meaning CASH, OVERBUNDANCE OF LIQUID while I was driving in the car with my daughter. What I mean by that is Cash is everything, and we should all strive for an overabundance of liquidity of money. One of the most important things is to have an emergency fund. Store your emergency fund in a Money Market Account for quick access in an emergency. The best ones are usually not at your traditional bank. You can compare the best ones with the best interest rates and with amenities like check writing privileges or a debit card on bankrate.com. Some people like Fidelity Money Market Account with the debit card, which is a good one. I like whoever gives me the best interest that is FDIC Insured. Most books say 3-6 months, but I have to be realistic it's hard for most people to do this. Especially during this covid pandemic or during tough times and unfortunately $1,000 as advised by Dave Ramsey will not cut it in these times but you have to start from somewhere. So, why not start by trying to save $1,000 first then any extra cash, throw it at the emergency fund until you reach your next $1,000, and then continue adding increasingly till you get to the min of 3 months. Then continue to save more.

You may be asking Paula where am I going to find this money? It is quite simple, CUT SOME STUFF! This is where a budget is handy. When you budget you can see where your money is going. Once again you can use an app, spreadsheet, or paper. Track everything you spend then you will know where to cut. Let's start slowly. Cut out coffee for a week or five days. A cheap coffee can cost about $2.99 a day well, that's if you buy only one cup. An expensive coffee from a high-end barista averages about $6.75 with all the frills. So, if you take $2.99 X 5 days = $14.95 or $6.75 X 5 days = $33.75. Now a week or five days can be done where you don't have this coffee once or twice a week. By the end of the month, the missed coffee purchases should add up to a week or five days. So, start small and use the savings from what you cut out and put it towards your emergency fund. We can even look at cutting out eating out. Consequently, for me eating out is a whole production. I can easily spend $100 on myself for 1 meal. Think about cutting out you're eating out for 2 weekends, again start slow. For me, that is 1 day usually Friday or Saturday where I would spend $100. That's $200 savings per month. Then increase your saving rate as you go. Take the train out slowly then run it off the tracks with steam of you increasing your momentum to save more.

Procrastination to start will always hold you back. If you procrastinate it will only delay your goal. Let's start today. Put away childish things and make a promise today to yourself that you will start TODAY. Every little bit helps you to reach your goal.

CHAPTER FIVE GIVING

Don't we learn to share in kindergarten? I think so. But I was an only child for my mother for a long time so there were not any siblings to share with. I do remember in middle school having friends and we shared and looked out for each other. For instance, if one person brought a hero aka a sub sandwich, and brought chips and a soda, we shared with each other. This was just how it was. I grew up with that mentally to share. But I did see my parents give to others. My mother gave money to my grandmother, and I learned to give. She also gave to less fortunate children and it prompted me as an adult to do the same. I remember in Florida when my daughter was attending school and there was a little girl who walked to school and my daughter shared, she did not have school supplies nor school uniforms. At that moment, I decided to buy the school supplies and uniforms for her.

As I stated earlier about my dad being a preacher, he always gave back. With his time and money to his parishioners. I recalled him going to nursing homes and bringing things for his parishioners. Also helping young men financially. My grandmother is also a preacher, and she took in many adults, and children who needed help. Another example is my aunts, I have one particular aunt who has always provided shelter and aid to anyone in need. So, I had good examples of how to give back. I have been on the receiving end of many blessings of others helping me and it is only right to give and help others. I do recall one of my ex-boyfriends he was always giving to strangers and displaced individuals living on the street and that left a good impression on me.

The saying what goes around comes back around also refers to giving if you are charitable, eventually, charity will come your way. This can be found in numerous scriptures in the Bible and when I went to World Changers, they preached about giving back.

2 Corinthians 9:7 – "Every man according as he purposeth in his heart,

so let him give; not grudgingly, or of necessity: for God loveth a cheerful giver."

Luke 6:38 – "Give, and it shall be given unto you."

2 Corinthians 9:6 – "But this I say, He which soweth sparingly shall reap also sparingly; and he which soweth bountifully shall reap also bountifully."

I really took these scriptures to heart. Therefore, in 2001 when I became a victim of the 9/11 disasters once I received numerous treatments, I decided this was my calling. That God saved my life so I should devote my life to giving back. So, I did, I thought the message from God since he blessed me by healing me and providing monetary provisions that if someone was in need, I needed to help them in a monetary way. Consequently, I gave money to many who asked. I also loaned money to many of my friends who asked and unfortunately, I got burned. They would not pay me back. No matter how many inquiries on when the monies would return to me.

I used to get so wounded by people taking advantage of my kindness but then I realized I did not have boundaries as far as how much I could give of myself to others. I then had to let those go, as leaves blow in the wind. I learned how to give back in other ways like volunteering and even housing exchange students in my home. Also, charity was for God and not for anyone. Therefore, I should not get broken when it was not reciprocated by the person I was helping. I then learned how to say No. Also, to move when God tells me to move. This was not a payback to God he does not do things for that. God does not bless you in that way.

I realized that when I looked around me even though I was giving of myself that God was blessing me in so many other ways. Do I give of myself for something in return from God? No, I give because my Bible tells me to, and it makes me feel good. This is where the cheerful giver part plays a major role. It should never be a burden to give and if you are giving under those pretenses, it is better to not give. Until your heart is whole and when you will not miss what you gave to others. This was a hard lesson to learn. But it is so freeing once you get it. When you have enough it's only right to help others who are suffering. I do not have the means to help everyone, and this is where boundaries play a major role. You have to know when to give and when to say No. Kind of like when you're flying on an airplane, they always tell you before takeoff "If you are traveling with a child or someone who requires assistance, secure your mask on first, and then assist the other person." You always must put yourself first then once you are ok then you can take care of anyone else.

As I have said before many people poured into me to make me what I am today, and I am so thankful. One of my favorite Aunts gave me shelter, another helped me pay for school. Some of my friends also gave me shelter, including my daughter's aunt. Of course, my parents always gave me when I was in need and even when I was not in need. Even recently my daughter gave me a monetary blessing. Within my workplace, I can name some of my peers and Supervisors who cheerfully gave to me. The most important thing is I am thankful and grateful, and I give God all the glory.

EPILOGUE/CONCLUSION

Every day is a lesson. So, when in doubt think back to who taught ya these valuable lessons about money and keep them in mind when they are good and in line with what I have shared. Put them into action. Remember you can manifest anything you want in life. Even getting a handle on your money. Let all your Challenges turn you into a Champion.

BIBLIOGRAPHY

U.S. Congress Publication date 2021 King James Bible Online Matthew King James Version (KJV) , OFFICIAL KING JAMES BIBLE ONLINE: AUTHORIZED KING JAMES VERSION (KJV)

Editor: Stephen Smith. Publication date: Sep 29, 2021. Publisher: OpenBible.info. https://www.openBible.info/topics/manifesting thoughts What Does the Bible Say About Fear and Anxiety? (openBible.info)

Fernandez, Elayna Best Bible Verses that Work with the Law of Attraction https://www.thepositivemom.com/law-of-attraction-Bible-verses

Bible Study Tools 2021 1 Corinthians 12:7-11 https://www.Biblestudytools.com/esv/1corinthians/passage/?q=1+corinthians+12:7-11

Rhonda Byrne The Secret New York ; London ; Toronto ; Sydney ; New Delhi : Atria Books ; Hillsboro, Oregon : Beyond Words Pub., 2006.

Ramsey, D. (2007). The Total Money Makeover: A proven plan for financial fitness. Nashville: Nelson Books.

Bach, D. (2003). The automatic millionaire: A powerful one-step plan to live and finish rich. Toronto: Doubleday Canada.

ABOUT THE AUTHOR

Paula Robertson Scott is an author, minister, teacher, and finance professional. Whose motto is that she wants everyone to win. She loves sharing and teaching others.

After being hurt in the 9/11 disaster she dedicated her life to helping others. Either thru volunteering her time or through monetary donations.

At age nine Paula gained an interest in finance. After loaning her older cousin twenty dollars and asking her to sign a contract with interest applied. Paula gained her Bachelor's degree in Business Administration and Master's degree in Organizational Management which led to her working in a variety of fields from retail, fine goods, healthcare, telecommunications, and finance.

Anything new Paula learns she always wants to share. Paula has a blended family and is a mother of 1 and stepmother of 2. She passionately believes in the power of Manifestation. She comes from humble beginnings and always puts God 1st in her life and everything she does. She has spread the gospel to her children, and she is a role model in showing them how to use what they have been taught to be better with their finances.

Made in the USA
Monee, IL
04 November 2026

67378040R00022